CAREER AS AN
ECONOMIST

ECONOMISTS APPLY ECONOMIC THEORIES and knowledge to determine how best to allocate resources. Those resources may include money, but can also include anything from crops to labor to clean air. They study, research, predict, and evaluate business and revenue trends in every industry and in every level of government.

The work itself involves considerable research and the collection of large amounts of data. Economists start with surveys, random samples, and statistical models. They study people's spending behavior, changing demographics, how scarce resources are distributed, and how various laws affect the economic health of individuals, organizations, and society as a whole. They also look at trends, both current and historical, prices, jobs, taxes, interest rates, and the financial markets. Sophisticated software is then used to analyze all the information they have amassed. Based on their evaluations, economists can predict future trends and recommend ways to improve outcomes in prices, productivity, employment rates, exports, and more. Their analyses and forecasts are frequently published in academic journal articles and other media sources.

Many economists work for the government. Economists employed by the federal government conduct the most surveys and collect most of the economic data in the US. They work in many different agencies, from the Department of Defense to the Department of the Interior. Their common goal is to assess current economic conditions and advise policy makers on how changes in legislation or public policy will affect the economy in the future. At the state and local level, government economists deal with issues such as income and sales taxes, minimum wage requirements, expansion of schools, and strengthening infrastructure.

Outside of government, economists work for all kinds of organizations and individuals. Businesses in every industry hire economists, but their advice is especially valuable to those with interests in other countries. Economists help companies determine what to sell, how much to produce, the selling price, staffing needs, what the competition is likely to do, and how consumer preferences will change over time. They also work for major international organizations such as the World Bank, International Monetary Fund, and the United Nations, where they study a variety of economic issues of global importance. There are also some economists at work in brokerage and investment firms, research firms, think tanks, and nonprofit organizations.

New economists can get started with a bachelor's degree, entering the field as research assistants or management trainees, but for most economist positions, a master's degree is required. To qualify for top chief economist jobs or to join a college faculty, a PhD is necessary. No matter how you cut it, there is a substantial investment in education. Is it worth it? Most economists say yes. They are paid an average annual salary of about $110,000, and the number employed is continuously rising. With an advanced degree and a few years in the field, it is possible to earn more than $175,000. Aside from good money, economists love the work, which is creative and intellectually stimulating. Economic conditions are constantly changing, making boredom very unlikely.

Economists are smart professionals with the innate ability to solve perplexing problems and pinpoint meaningful details. They are great with puzzles and are obsessed with finding patterns and trends. If this sounds like you, then you may have what it takes to be an economist.

WHAT YOU CAN DO NOW

A CAREER IN ECONOMICS REQUIRES at least four years of college. Start preparing for college entrance requirements and standardized tests right away. Plan your high school curriculum carefully to make sure you meet all the admission requirements for any colleges you are considering. These requirements may vary, but math is the backbone of this field. Take as many math classes as possible, especially those dealing with statistics. Economists also write many reports and give presentations. These tasks will be easier if you prepare with communications classes like speech, debate, and English. Other helpful classes include social science, computer applications, current events, and a foreign language. Many economists work abroad for international organizations where they interact with people who might not speak fluent English.

Learn more about what this career is really like. Your guidance counselor can help by inviting an economist to speak on career day or arrange for a job shadowing opportunity. Be prepared with plenty of questions. Ask about the pros and cons of their work and what advice they have to offer. If you live near a college or university, contact the economics department and arrange for a visit. Talk to as many professors and students as you can. Any of these activities will provide a better idea of what an economist really does and whether it is the type of work that you would like to do.

The field of economics is segmented into a number of specializations. You can learn more about them by joining local branches of national economics associations and doing research on the Internet. If you find a niche that is interesting, consider taking some classes that are related to that specialization.

Things change fast in the world of economics. Get in the habit of staying up to date on economic trends by reading business and trade magazines. Professional associations are also an excellent source of economic news.

Admissions officers and employers like to see evidence of leadership skills and community involvement. You can demonstrate both by joining the economics club or a community service organization, and by participating in student government.

HISTORY OF THE CAREER

THE HISTORY OF ECONOMIC THOUGHT and the people who put forth theories on the subject can be traced back to ancient times. In China, Fan Li (517 BC), an advisor to King Goujian of Yue, wrote on economic issues and developed a set of golden rules for business. Chanakya (350 BC) is known as the father of economics in India. While serving as a royal advisor, he wrote the Arthashastra, a political treatise on economic policy and military strategy. His work is considered an important precursor to classical economics.

Ancient Greek philosophers also made important contributions to the body of economic thought. In *The Republic* (380 BC), Plato wrote about economic justice and referenced such ideas as specialization of labor in an ideal city-state. Plato was also the first to advocate the credit theory of money. In response to Plato's blueprint of a society based on common ownership of resources, Aristotle mused about the wisdom of wealth acquisition and questioned whether property should be in private or public stewardship. He reasoned that the oligarchical form of state endorsed by Plato should not be in complete control of resources due to the "wickedness of human nature."

The Middle Ages was a time when religious belief dominated philosophical conversations. For example, scholar and economic writer, Thomas Aquinas, contended that businesses had the moral obligation to sell goods at a just price to maintain the social order. In his treatise, *Summa Theologica*, he defined a just price as being sufficient to cover the costs of production and living wages for a worker and his family. Aquinas further argued that price gouging in time of extreme consumer need was immoral.

Mercantilism dominated Europe from the 16th to the 18th century. It was a time in which medieval feudalism waned while explorers like Christopher Columbus opened up new opportunities for trade with the New World and Asia. Mercantilism was an economic theory that favored commercialism and profitable trading. Advocates of the theory believed that international trade could not benefit all countries equally, therefore, the state should protect local markets and supply sources through the use of tariffs and military action. In short, it planted the seed of protectionism as we know it today.

In the Western world, economics began as a distinct discipline in the 19th century during the Industrial Revolution and the Great Divergence, both of which greatly accelerated economic growth in the West. There were many Western economists who made major contributions to the financial and social history of the United States. One of the first was Adam Smith (1723-1790), who is known as the father of modern political economy. His famous four-volume compendium, *The Wealth of Nations,* was one of the earliest publications to address economic growth in a world gone global. In it, Smith laid out his vision of a free market economy based on secure property, accumulation of capital, and widening markets. Growth, he said, was especially dependent on the increasing division of labor. Smith was very much against mercantilism with its protectionism, tariffs, and hoarding of hard assets that prevailed at the time. Attempting to regulate all negative human actions, he argued, was not only futile, but detrimental to economic growth.

David Ricardo (1772-1823), a classical economist known for his Iron Law of Wages, took an interest in economics after reading Smith's *The Wealth of Nations* in 1799. Ricardo was a wildly successful stock and real estate speculator who believed that protectionism was not in the best interests of any nation. His best-known publication, *On the Principles of Political Economy and Taxation* (1817), was a critique of barriers to international trade. It also described how income should be distributed in the population. Ricardo contended that workers should receive a livable wage and that landowners who exploited labor through rents were not fostering a greater society. His book was used as the standard text on economics by universities well into the beginning of the 20th century.

Neoclassical economics emerged in the 1870s. It was an approach to economics that focused on supply and demand to determine prices, output, and the ability to maximize profit. Alfred Marshall (1842-1924), the first professor of economics at the University of Cambridge, was a dominant figure in this line of thought. His most important work, *Principles of Economics,* emphasized that the price and production of goods are determined by both supply and demand – a radical concept at the time. Marshall is also credited with turning economics into a science rather than a philosophy by applying rigorous mathematics methods.

By the 20th century, the Industrial Revolution had resulted in an exponential increase in the consumption of resources. The corresponding rise in wealth and population was viewed as great progress. Then came the Great Depression and unprecedented upheaval in the world economy that led to huge Wall Street loses and mass unemployment in the US. After nearly being wiped out himself, the great economist John Maynard Keynes (1883-1946) wrote the seminal book *General Theory of Employment, Interest and Money.* While orthodox economists were calling for austerity measures, Keynes argued that deficit spending was the best way to kick-start economic recovery. The book laid the foundation for modern macroeconomics.

One of the most influential economists of the 20th century was Milton Friedman (1912-2006). Friedman worked on the New Deal, a series of programs designed by President Franklin D. Roosevelt to provide relief from the effects of the Great Depression. While Friedman was in favor of the New Deal, he opposed most government intervention in general and price controls in particular. He is best known for promoting free markets as the way to create political and social freedom. Friedman won the Nobel Prize in Economic Sciences in 1976.

In 2008, another financial crisis led to a global recession, now known as the Great Recession. Economists argued over what should be done, but as the US economy teetered on the edge of collapse, a consensus emerged in favor of Keynesian solutions. In October of 2008, as unemployment began to climb, the US rolled out stimulus plans designed to get the economy back on track. Some European countries followed suit, but others responded with strict austerity measures. In 2010, the rising public debt in the US was viewed by many as the problem and further stimulus plans, such as major public works programs, were put on the back burner. The result was an economy that was recovering, but at a stubbornly sluggish rate. By 2016, several nations swung the other way, from austerity to Keynesian economics. Only time will tell which economic theory is better in times of economic crises.

WHERE YOU WILL WORK

THERE ARE AROUND 21,500 ECONOMISTS working in the US. Most are located in large cities, particularly in business trade centers like New York and San Francisco, or capital cities such as Washington and Phoenix. There are few jobs in rural areas, except on campuses of large universities which may be located there.

Some economists work abroad. They are usually employed by large companies engaged in global commerce or by federal government agencies that deal with international trade policies. Other employers include international organizations such as the World Bank, International Monetary Fund, and the United Nations.

About a third of all economists are employed by various government agencies. The federal government employs more than state and local agencies, with the bulk of the hiring done by the Department of Commerce and Department of Labor. An equal number of economists work in private industry. Most are employed by banks, insurance companies, technical consulting firms, scientific research and development services, and management consulting firms.

Many economists work in academia. Most are on the faculties of colleges and universities, but the numbers who teach economics at the high school level is growing steadily.

Some economists are independent consultants. In fact, it is quite common for economists to combine a full-time job in government, academia, or business with consulting work on the side. Faculty economists, in particular, often enjoy flexible work schedules that leave time for occasional consulting projects.

Economists typically work independently in a well-appointed office. For some, that means a home office. Travel may be required to do fieldwork or to attend meetings and professional conferences.

Most economists work full time. Part-time work is common, though it is usually an adjunct to a full-time job. Work schedules vary, but most are based on a typical 40-hour workweek.

THE WORK YOU WILL DO

ECONOMISTS STUDY HOW LIMITED RESOURCES are utilized to fulfill needs within a variety of areas, such as business development, education, health, and the environment. They look at how money, land, labor, and raw materials are allocated, and whether current policies are effective or changes need to be made. Some economists may be concerned with the cost of products or energy. Others may deal with issues like business cycles or exchange rates. All economists base their conclusions on data and research.

Economists obtain evidence through various means, including surveys, random samples, and statistical models. They also monitor economic trends and study historical trends. Collected data is analyzed by using a variety of software programs, including spreadsheets, statistical analysis, and database management programs. The findings are then used to develop forecasts of what is likely to happen in the future with or without changes in current policies.

There are two basic types of economists: macro and micro.

Macroeconomics deals with the economy as a whole, rather than individual markets. Macroeconomists, also known as monetary economists, research long-term trends related to unemployment, inflation, and economic growth throughout history. They may study fiscal and monetary policies of regional, national, and global economies to determine the effects of money supply and interest rates on unemployment, inflation, investments, and productivity.

Microeconomics is concerned with the economic decisions of companies or individuals. Microeconomists primarily analyze supply and demand decisions to determine how to maximize productivity, how much demand there will be for certain products, and the ideal pricing of products or services. Some microeconomists are tasked with analyzing the effects of government actions, such as tax cuts and budget deficits, on business.

Daily duties of economists can vary greatly depending on the type of employer and the purpose of the work, but general tasks include the following:

- Determine the best methods for collecting data

- Create and conduct surveys

- Use software and advanced mathematical models to interpret data

- Test the effectiveness of current policies for the allocation of resources

- Analyze and forecast market trends

- Prepare reports, tables, and charts

- Deliver oral presentations of research findings

- Make recommendations for changes in economic policies

- Provide economic advice to businesses and governments

- Write articles for academic journals and other media sources

An economist's work can be applied to many different fields, but these can be roughly broken down into four main sectors: government, corporate, finance, and academic.

Government economists are employed by various agencies at every level of government.

Their primary responsibility is to gather and analyze data from numerous sectors of the economy to prepare economic forecasts. Data might include employment rates, wholesale prices, total retail sales, new housing starts, wages, and industry growth. Their findings may be used to project government-spending needs or to prepare annual budgets, among other things. Government economists also study the economic impact of current or proposed legislation or policies, such as trade regulations, interest rates, or the budget deficit.

Corporate economists work in research organizations and private institutions.

They are able to make accurate predictions by working with many different statistics, compiling large databases, and recognizing trends. Typical responsibilities include conducting market research, projecting consumer demand, studying competitors, and assessing the economy of countries where expansion might be possible. They may also evaluate the effect of government policies, such as tariffs, minimum wage requirements, antitrust laws, and international trade. They advise management on the effects that current policies and new legislation could have on the company.

Financial economists study financial markets and analyze savings, investments, and risk for financial institutions, including banks, exchanges, brokerages, mutual funds, hedge funds, and others.

For example, they might evaluate the payout from issuing certain types of loans to different categories of customers. They also study the effect of changing interest rates on banking systems. The data they collect and analyze is used to explain economic problems that affect the institution they work for and make recommendations on how to best deal with them.

Academic economists work in universities and colleges, and high schools.

Their work falls into two categories: teaching and research. Professors at the college level may teach advanced economics subjects to students who will become future economists. Teachers in high school help students understand basic economic concepts and introduce simple analytical tools. College professors are expected to conduct research projects designed to answer economic policy questions of interest. For example, they might suggest changes to the Social Security system that would better ensure the program's long-term sustainability. Academic economists often publish books and articles for academic journals.

All economists are familiar with general principles that can be applied to a wide variety of industries, such as medicine, education, law, energy, and environmental protection. In fact, economics is such a broad field of study, most economists specialize in specific areas. There are many specializations to choose from, and these are the most common.

Labor economists are concerned with employment levels and how wages are set. They look at trends in salary and study the supply of workers versus the demand for labor by employers. They are often referred to as demographic economists because of the type of data they use. For example, they may study how different generations, such as Baby Boomers or Millennials, affect unemployment rates or wage levels. Labor economists also look at the effects of labor-related organizations (such as unions) and government policies.

Agricultural economists apply their economic knowledge and skills to farming and land development issues.

Their primary focus is on resource management and allocation. In an agricultural setting, resources include land, farm equipment, livestock, and natural resources, such as coal, fresh water, and natural gas. The goal is to maximize resources in a way that promotes sustainable success. Some agricultural economists work at a desk, reading reports, tracking economic trends, and performing calculations. Others work in the field, interviewing farmers, surveying land, and looking at the layouts and outputs of rural and farming communities. A few work with legislatures, often lobbying governments on behalf of farmers.

International economists are primarily interested in global financial markets and exchange rates.

They look at international markets and study the effects of tariffs, trade restrictions, and currency exchange rates. They may examine how these issues impact particular business concerns or the country's entire economy.

Energy economists are interested in topics related to the supply and use of energy.

Their work is usually on a worldwide scale, including issues such as global energy supplies and demands, climate change, politics, indigenous rights, and sustainability. Research may focus on traditional sources of energy like coal and petroleum products, or on alternative supplies like wind and solar energy. National governments use their findings to make policy and work with allies, but energy economists also work for private companies, research institutions, and academic organizations.

Environmental economists are interested in how the production, transport, and use of resources affects the environment.

For example, they might study how coal-fired power plants cause pollution or what happens to watersheds and fisheries when hydroelectric dams are put in place. They are responsible for calculating the cost of environmental impacts to determine if production is financially sustainable, or needs to be adjusted to limit environmental costs.

STORIES OF ECONOMISTS AT WORK

I Am a Chief Economist for a Bank

"Because my bank is located on the West Coast, my day starts early. By 5:00 a.m. I am reading the breaking news from the financial centers on the East Coast and reviewing the economic reports from Washington DC. When a major report is released, I write a brief analysis on what the new data means for the markets, the Federal Reserve's monetary policy, and the economic outlook in general. I email that to my colleagues and media contacts. Next, I meet with my executive team and brief them on economic trends that could affect our bank's clients.

The rest of my day is a combination of analytical activities and meetings. I spend a considerable amount of time preparing for upcoming presentations. People would be surprised at how much public speaking an economist does. Any economics major should take some public speaking classes and get some presentation training. Every day, clients, prospects, and reporters are asking me questions about the economy and its drivers. I need to break down some very complicated issues and explain them in a way they can understand. I especially enjoy pointing out how it impacts their personal financial situations.

My advice to economics majors is to jump in and get some work experience as soon as possible. What you learn in class is theory. How you apply that knowledge in the real world is the exciting part. I worked as a part-time research assistant while working towards my master's. What I learned doing that was invaluable."

I Am a Litigation Consultant

"One of the best things about pursuing a career in economics is the great variety of different careers paths to choose from. You can become a straight economist, or you can be a sociologist, management consultant, or investment analyst. I was always interested in the law so that is the direction I chose.

As a litigation consultant, I spend most of my time reading all kinds of documents and studying up about cases. I also run numerical models to quantify some aspect of a case or to help determine what a suit's value is. In most cases, I will be called on to be an expert witness. A lot of work goes into that before I get on the stand. I really need to know my facts because someone will be trying hard to disprove some of the things I'm saying.

The most rewarding part of this work is helping people.

Lawsuits can be very stressful and contentious. When I can provide a positive step towards resolution, it's a good feeling. I also enjoy problem solving, but solving puzzles can also be the most challenging aspect. It requires a lot of study and lateral thinking to come up with the right answer.

My advice for anyone considering a career in economics is to get as much advice as you can. Ideally, you would have a mentor, but you can get a lot of help from school career counselors. They know what they're talking about and they're there to help you. They can get you placed in internships and help you understand the various different paths you can go down as an economist."

I Am a Land-Use Economist

"Most people think economists work for major banks or Wall Street firms or big federal government agencies, but economists have so many more choices. I work for a real estate and urban planning consulting firm. My specialty is analyzing the fiscal and economic impacts of high-level urban development at the local and regional levels. For example, if a developer wants to build 1,000 new houses in Maricopa County, Arizona, I would be asked to calculate the total tax revenues that would be generated by the new residents. Then I would compare those projected revenues to the county's cost of providing services, such as schools, water, and public safety.

Most of my day is spent alone with my computer, collecting and analyzing socioeconomic data, running complex calculations, and doing project feasibility studies. There is more to my job than number crunching though. At least two hours a day (on average) are spent presenting my findings to clients. My college professors warned me early on that communications skills were just as important as math and computer skills. They were so right! I can't emphasize enough the importance of not just being a good writer, but also being able to write quickly, concisely, and in a compelling way that focuses on the most relevant information. Readers can easily get lost in economic jargon and that doesn't help anybody. I also read a lot. Academic journals and financial newspapers keep me abreast of current topics relevant to my field."

PERSONAL QUALIFICATIONS

ARE YOU A MATH WHIZ? IF YOU ACED calculus, statistics, and other advanced math classes, that is a good start. All economists have a passion for numbers and enjoy using them to solve problems and predict future trends. Here are some other personal traits that successful economists have in common.

Successful economists are great thinkers. Every day they use logic and higher-level reasoning to solve complex problems. Although they generally take a systematic approach based on critical thinking, they also have to be creative. The best economists look at the data from different angles and think outside of the box to arrive at the most accurate conclusions.

Analytical skills are a must-have for this work. Economists are constantly collecting and scrutinizing even the tiniest bits of information. They mentally organize data into trends and patterns that complete a puzzle. Every detail is important to ensure accuracy in their findings. In fact, being detail oriented is perhaps the most important skill of all. Every detail matters and can change the big picture. It requires a high level of nitpicking not seen in many other careers.

Good communications skills are a must. Economists write many reports for colleagues and clients. Some also write for publication in journals or for news media. Nearly all have to present their findings in writing at some point. Your writing must be clear and concise so readers can understand it. Speaking skills are also important. Economists frequently explain their work to others through live presentations. When economists talk to each other, it sounds like gobbledygook to most outsiders. But very often they have to explain economic concepts to people without a background in economics. Getting relevant points across requires clear, simple language.

Good economists are equally comfortable working alone or as part of a team. Most of their time is spent on independent research, preparing statistical charts, and writing reports. While working independently, it is important to be self-motivated and disciplined. On some large projects or when there is a mountain of research involved, economists work in teams. In that situation, it is important to view other team members as partners and work in a spirit of collaboration.

Strict deadlines are a fact of life for most economists. Most of the time, working hours are predictable and regular, but when a deadline is looming, it may be necessary to work overtime. The pressure to get things done can get intense. Successful economists are able to stay focused and do not let the stress get to them.

ATTRACTIVE FEATURES

SUCCESSFUL ECONOMISTS LOVE WHAT THEY DO and are rarely bored. The work is very creative and intellectually stimulating. Plus, they get to work with all kinds of smart and interesting people. Here are the other good reasons for pursuing this career.

Economists receive nice dividends for their work. It is a high-paying career with an average annual salary of almost $110,000 – a number that is rising steadily. Even those who enter the field through a side door are well compensated. Economists taking jobs as market research analysts, statisticians, and financial analysts, can expect to earn $70,000, $80,000, and $90,000, respectively. Economists working as actuaries, for example, are paid salaries averaging $107,000, while political scientists earn roughly the same at $105,000. Keep in mind that education and experience matter. With a graduate degree and some professional experience, successful economists earn more than $175,000.

Economists have many choices regarding the type of work they want to do. They may work in a variety of specialized fields, such as financial, labor, and tech. There are also many different types of work regardless of the industry. For example, econometricians study economic phenomena, while macroeconomists evaluate how markets function. Behavioral economists observe how economic decisions are affected by cognitive and emotional factors, while international economists analyze trade between nations. Financial economists study saving and investing, while public finance economists analyze the role of governments in the economic process.

There can be considerable career mobility for professional economists who have some experience. An economist's knowledge and skills can easily be transferred from one work setting to another. For example, an economist working for a private consulting firm could take advantage of opportunities in a state government agency, a trade association, a think tank, a lobbying group, or an international nonprofit organization.

Do you dream of traveling the world? Economists work in some of the most exciting cities in the world. In fact, many economists report that traveling to different countries is one of the most enjoyable aspects of their job. You can explore the world and immerse yourself in other cultures, all while earning a very good income. College students, take note: These travel opportunities are usually offered only to those who are fluent in a foreign language.

UNATTRACTIVE ASPECTS

PROFESSIONAL ECONOMISTS ARE GENERALLY HAPPY with their career choice, but no job is perfect. There are advantages and disadvantages to pursuing a career as an economist. Here is the downside.

It is a small universe. With only about 22,000 jobs available nationwide, the competition to land one of them can be tough. The forecast for the future is not reassuring either. Job growth for economists is only projected to be six percent within the coming decade. That is about the same as the national growth rate for all US occupations, but it is not great. Most new graduates will not be able to start out as an economist. Instead, they need to apply their skills to other jobs that are closely related. For example, one might look for a job as a market research analyst. That occupation is projected to grow by over 40 percent through 2020 – much better! Other possibilities include jobs for actuaries, which will grow by almost 30 percent, and financial analyst jobs, which will increase by over 20 percent. You will have to be careful about which occupations show the most promise though. While economists are well versed in statistics, for example, statisticians will experience only a 14 percent increase in demand for their services.

The educational requirements to be an economist are high, and employers are continually raising the bar. A bachelor's degree is the absolute minimum and at best, that will only get a new economist an entry-level position as an assistant. Without a graduate degree, it will be very difficult to move up the career ladder. Most jobs today require several additional years in school to complete either a master's degree or a PhD in economics. In addition, this career is only for those who have a strong aptitude for math. For those who do not relish the thought of using statistics, calculus, and other advanced math concepts to perform economic analyses every day, this career is a bad choice.

The work of economists is not without pressure. Although they work regular hours most of the time, deadlines, tight schedules, and heavy workloads are common. When strict deadlines are looming, overtime is likely to be required. It can be hard to keep up with your assignments when there are numerous interruptions throughout the day from people wanting more data. There are also many meetings and conferences, which can push the workday into overtime.

EDUCATION AND TRAINING

A BACHELOR'S DEGREE ALONE MAY BE ENOUGH to qualify for some entry-level jobs, including jobs with the government. Working for the federal government requires at least a bachelor's degree with 21 hours of economics and at least three hours of advanced mathematics. Requirements for other jobs are less specific. The degree does not necessarily need to be in economics. A major in business management or a math-related field, such as statistics is acceptable. Students majoring in areas other than economics should load up on math courses, computer science, history, political science, and law. They should also learn how to prepare presentations.

Undergraduate degrees in economics are offered by many schools. Most programs include at least 10 courses on economic subjects, including microeconomics, macroeconomics, econometrics, sampling theory, survey design, and the history of economic thought. Math skills are extremely important in this profession. At a minimum, economics majors take at least two math classes, statistics and calculus.

Advanced Education

Most government and private business employers of economists want to see candidates that have earned a graduate degree. In today's complex world, an undergraduate degree simply does not provide all that is needed to be a full-fledged economist. A bachelor's degree in economics can get you a job as a data analyst at an insurance company, but a master's degree will qualify you to be a chief economist with an international organization. The step up is well worth the additional one or two years of study.

A PhD in economics is the best way to demonstrate you are a serious candidate for high-level economist positions. Programs vary from school to school, but it takes five to six years of study on average to earn a doctoral degree focused on detailed research in specialty fields. There are numerous specialties to choose from, such as advanced economic theory, demographic economics, international economics, agricultural economics, and labor economics. Any student who aims to pursue a PhD should research the possibilities carefully while studying for a master's degree. A good way to do this is through informational interviews. By talking to people in all different areas of economics, you will learn what real jobs are out there and what they are really like. You will probably learn about specializations that you did not even know existed.

To join the faculty at a secondary school or community college, a master's degree is usually sufficient. At a large college or university, however, an applicant generally will need a PhD.

Hands-On Training

Employers like to see some kind of real world experience on a résumé. One way to get it is through an internship. Most colleges with economics departments help students find internships. In fact, they encourage students to participate in several programs within different industries to get a view of the possibilities. Interns typically gather and analyze data, research economic issues and trends, conduct interviews or surveys, and write reports on their findings. These are the very same tasks involved in most entry-level jobs. In addition to valuable experience, internships provide a great way to make contacts that could lead to full-time employment.

Other ways to get experience include assisting a professor or by getting a part-time job. For experience that is balanced, it is advantageous to work both in the private sector and in the government. Any experience working in business or finance can be beneficial.

EARNINGS

ECONOMISTS ARE PAID WELL AND SALARIES in this field are growing steadily. The average yearly salary for economists is close to $110,000. That works out to about $50 per hour. The most successful economists make out even better, averaging more than $175,000 per year. Even those who graduate with just a bachelor's degree can expect a relatively high starting salary. Actual earnings though depend on location, type of employer, job title, and level of education.

Location

Most economists live and work in large cities. Not surprisingly, the city-dwellers are going to make more money than economists in rural areas, but not all cities are created equal. The highest salaries are found in San Francisco, Bethesda, Austin, Washington DC, Los Angeles, New York, Stamford, St. Louis, Pittsburgh, and Baltimore. Salaries vary among states, too. In general, the lowest salaries are in the Mountain and Southern regions while the highest are in the Mid-Atlantic and Southwest. More specifically, the top states for economists are as follows:

Arizona $147,000

Virginia $117,000

District of Columbia $116,000

Maryland $110,000

California $103,000

Top-paying employers and industries

The type of employer who hires you also plays a big role in what you can expect to earn as an economist. Based solely on income, the best industry to get into is securities and investment banking. The pay for entry-level jobs is getting close to the six-figure threshold, and the average is around $150,000. Other good choices in private industry include scientific research and development services and technical consulting services.

Economists can also do well financially working for the federal government. The average annual salary for economists employed by the federal government is $115,000, which is above the overall average. The federal government has agencies that hire economists all over the country. Those who are paid the most, however, work in and around the Washington DC metro area. Salaries also depend on the importance of the agency. For example, the Federal Reserve is probably the highest level of a federal agency employing economists. Economists working there are paid an average salary of almost $150,000, which is about the same as the top-paying private industry.

Education

Like most professions, income for economists rises with the level of education. The average earnings for economists with a bachelor's degree range from $45,000 to $75,000. While this is at the lower end of the pay scale, it is a respectable income for a four-year investment. Most individuals who enter the field with a bachelor's degree work in jobs with titles other than economist. Salaries will vary depending on the job title. A business analyst, for example, will earn an average of $57,000 per year while a research analyst can expect $80,000. Schools also make a difference. Graduates from the University of Washington earn salaries in the range of $40,000 to $65,000 while the range for those who attended the University of Massachusetts is $55,000 to $125,000. This school preference is less pronounced as economists gain more education and experience.

Most employers prefer candidates with advanced degrees, and they are willing to pay for it. In fact, it is listed in the top five careers that pay the highest return for a master's degree. The additional step up in education is worth an extra $10,000 in starting pay.

The average base salary for economists increases with every level of educational attainment. At the top is a PhD, with salaries ranging from $70,000 to $175,000. Most professionals with doctoral degrees who work in major cities enjoy salaries in the six-figure range. Here are some examples:

- San Francisco $154,000
- New York $135,000
- Baltimore $121,000
- Seattle $117,000
- Washington DC $104,000

Professionals holding doctoral degrees in this field generally pursue careers as chief economists or in academia. Chief economists do a lot better than associate professors – more than $40,000 a year more in earnings.

It is not uncommon for economists to supplement their incomes with part-time jobs. In fact, one out of four economists take in an additional $10,000 a year from side employment. Some teach, others write books and articles, and many do occasional consulting work.

Economists who work full time for the government or for private companies receive benefits. Typical benefits packages include paid holidays and vacations, health insurance, and retirement plans.

OPPORTUNITIES

JOB GROWTH FOR ECONOMISTS IS PROJECTED to increase about six percent over the next 10 years. That is in line with the average for all occupations. The most growth will occur in private industry, especially in the areas of scientific research, tech, and consulting.

The higher demand for the services of economists in the private sector is based on several factors:

- Increasing complexity of a world economy
- More intense competition in the global marketplace
- More business decisions are being based on carefully researched quantitative analysis
- Additional financial regulations

Jobs for economists are turning up in a growing array of businesses, but the highest demand should be in management, scientific services, and tech companies. Some of the most interesting employers are located in Silicon Valley, where top tech companies are hiring chief economists – and even entire economic teams – at a very rapid pace. It is a great time for economists with PhDs to consider the tech industry, but there is also a wide variety of roles for junior economists. In addition to traditional data crunching roles, these less educated professionals are sought to work in corporate strategy or on policy teams.

Professional consulting services are continuing to grow in popularity among US businesses. As the number of economist specialties widens, so do the number of opportunities. Many corporations prefer to hire economic consultants rather than keeping a full-time economist on staff. This is not just a cost-saving measure. Corporate employers like to be able to tap the expertise of economists in varying specialties as the needs arise. The greatest demand for consultants is in micro and macro -economics, finance, and labor.

Economists are also needed in all kinds of nonprofit organizations. Some of the largest employers are unions, chambers of commerce, and think tanks. Those with good communications skills are especially needed because after analyzing issues, it is necessary to explain them in ways that can be understood by the average citizen as well as government officials who are responsible for making and implementing policy.

Public Sector Jobs

Government agencies, especially at the federal level, have historically been major sources of jobs for economists. That is expected to change, however. Over the next 10 years, anticipated reductions in federal spending are expected to have a negative impact on jobs for economists. How much of a decrease to expect is unclear. On the bright side, economists are less likely to be the victims of downsizing than most other federal government jobs. At the same time, employment for economists in state and local governments is expected to rise. One area of growing demand is in secondary schools. Until recently, the subject of economics was not introduced until the third or fourth year of high school. That has definitely changed. Economics has become an increasingly important and popular high school course, and there is an increasing demand for teachers who are qualified to teach economics to younger students.

Educational Advantages and Differences

Applicants with a bachelor's degree can expect to face very strong competition for jobs. As a result, they will likely need to look for their first jobs outside the standard economist occupation. The least competitive job titles include research assistants, financial analysts, market analysts, survey designers, and business consultants.

Job seekers with a master's degree or PhD will have the best prospects. These highly trained individuals will be in a good position to compete for top economist jobs, both in the public and private sectors. The only exception may be for those seeking professorships or tenures at universities. The high pay and exceptional job security that accompanies those jobs attracts many qualified candidates.

GETTING STARTED

LAY DOWN THE FOUNDATION FOR YOUR CAREER as soon as you enter college. Carefully plan your courses, extracurricular activities, and employment in a way that will best showcase your abilities and interests. Aggressively pursue scholarships and other honorary opportunities. They can make the difference between landing a great job and finding one that is merely satisfactory. It tells prospective employers that others have evaluated your qualifications and found them impressive.

Take advantage of internship opportunities. In addition to invaluable real-world experience, they offer excellent networking opportunities. Nurture every one. The world of economics is a small one, and the future of your career may well depend on who you have impressed. In some cases, companies use internships to screen and recruit future employees.

When you are ready to start your job search, start with your professors and the placement office at your college. Look for job postings and upcoming career fairs. Ask to be included on career network emails that the school sends out. Sometimes recruiters visit campuses. Do not miss out on making connections just because you did not know about the event in time. Openings for economists are often listed in professional journals and on the websites of professional organizations. You can also apply directly to colleges, or government agencies that hire economists. Make sure your résumé is polished, and be ready to tailor it for each organization you submit it to.

Think outside the box. You will quickly learn that most economist jobs do not have "economist" in the job title. This can make it seem like there are very few jobs available. The trick is to find jobs that are not tagged economics. You will need to get familiar with the many different job titles that are associated with your career path. You will likely get more results from searching for market research assistant, actuary, or credit analyst. At the beginning, take any job that can use your skills to get you started. Be creative and brainstorm the possibilities. For example, are you a master of social media? Google, Facebook, and all the other tech giants have economists on board to analyze user data. In fact, tech companies – especially start-ups – are a great hunting ground for jobs that will use your skills.

Consider teaching part time. Plenty of economists with higher degrees do this to supplement their income, keep up-to-date with trends, and participate in research. It takes a master's degree to teach in community colleges and in high schools. A PhD is required to teach at the university level. You can test your teaching skills by tutoring or mentoring. The pay may not be great, but it will look good on your résumé. Plus, it is a good way to hone your communications skills.

Stay current. Make a routine of reading local, regional, and international news. You should be constantly reading – newspapers, magazines, and websites. Be ready for job interviews by knowing what other economists are projecting.

ASSOCIATIONS

■ **American Economic Association**
https://www.aeaweb.org/resources/students/careers

■ **National Association for Business Economics**
http://www.nabe.com

■ **National Association of Forensic Economics**
http://nafe.net

■ **Council for Economic Education**
http://councilforeconed.org

■ **Association for Evolutionary Economics**
http://afee.net

■ **Association of Environmental and Resource Economists**
http://www.aere.org

■ **American Agricultural Economic Association**
www.aaea.org

■ **The American Real Estate and Urban Economics Association**
www.areuea.org

PERIODICALS

■ **The Economist**
http://www.economist.com

■ **The American Economic Review**
http://www.aeaweb.org/aer/contents/index.php

WEBSITES

■ **EconJobs**
https://www.econ-jobs.com

■ **AEA Jobs**
https://www.aeaweb.org

■ **Bureau of Economic Analysis**
http://www.bea.gov

■ Economagic
http://www.economagic.com

www.ingramcontent.com/pod-product-compliance
Lightning Source LLC
Chambersburg PA
CBHW061237180526
45170CB00003B/1337